BIR~ ~
FA~

Text by

PETER HAWKEY
Warden/Naturalist of the Farne Islands

Drawn by

RONALD EMBLETON, R.O.I.

ISBN 0 946928 37 1

© 1990

First published 1973
This (revised) edition 1990

Published by
BUTLER PUBLISHING
Cliffside, Rothbury, Northumberland NE65 7YG

Printed by
MAYFAIR PRINTERS LTD
William Street, Sunderland, Tyne & Wear SR1 1UL

THE FARNES

The Farne Islands, which are chiefly naked rocks, varying in number from 15 to 28 according to the state of the tide, take their name from the largest which lies nearest to the mainland.

The name Farne is derived from the Celtic "ferann" meaning "land". From an ancient document we find that the names of the islands were almost the same in the 13th century as today. They are the most easterly proportion of the Great Whin Sill. This formation of igneous rock runs from High Forces on the Tees through Durham and Northumberland reaching the sea coast at Cullernose Point where it appears as a vertical cliff. It then bends northward forming the rocks of the coastline as far as Dunstanburgh Castle. It reappears at Embleton and then leaves the mainland forming the Farne Islands. It re-enters the mainland at Bamburgh Castle. The Whin Sill is mainly hard dolerite of about 100 feet thickness, columnar and fissured. The columnar from the sea on the south cliff of the Farnes as well as at the Pinnacles which three in number, are to be found on the south-east of Staple Island. Large fissures can be seen on the Inner Farne at St. Cuthbert's Gut and the Churn. At the Churn, when a storm rises, the water rushes up the channel and rises through a 'blow hole' to a height of one hundred feet.

A number of the rocks are rounded due to glacial action and deposits of boulder clay on the Inner Farne, Staple Island, Brownsman and the West Wideopens have created layers of soil which are rich from bird droppings. Sedimentary rocks can only be found on the Brownsman, the Bridges and Nameless Rock.

There are no trees on the islands but a few elder bushes, introduced by the lighthouse keepers, can be seen on the Inner Farne. Although the area of soil is very small there is a wide variety of vegetation. Sea campion is the characteristic plant of the islands and it blooms in the summer months. More than 70 plants grow on the Farnes as well as lichens and mosses. The orange flowered *Amsinckia intermedia*, a native of California, is found in a fair sized area of the Inner Farne, accidentally introduced by the keepers among poultry feed many years ago.

Although Aidan was the first to live as a hermit on the island it was the prolonged sojourn of St. Cuthbert which made the islands famous. He was followed by a number of hermits about whom little is known apart from the host of miracles which took the place of history in those primitive times. The first was Ethelwald, a monk of Ripon, who lived there from 687 to 699. He was succeeded by Felgeld, for whom Bishop Eadfrid rebuilt Cuthbert's oratory. The next hermit was Elwin who left after a quarrel with one Bartholomew who had also come to live there. After living alone for a while Bartholomew was joined by Thomas de Melsonby, who had been elected Prior of Durham against the wishes of Henry III, and had to take refuge in Farne for his own safety. At first the two hermits quarrelled but after a time lived amicably together.

In the "Life of Bartholomew" written about this time there is an interesting account of the islands. It says that "of the adjacent islands, one supplies hay, another fuel, another (which is the nearest) serves as a burial place for shipwrecked sailors. Here the demons are believed to reside, who were compelled by St. Cuthbert to quit his island. The brethren, when enjoying their rest after labour, have seen them on a sudden, clad in cowls and riding upon goats black in complexion, short in stature, their countenances most hideous their heads long the appearance of the whole troop horrible. Like soliders they brandished in their hands lances, which they darted after the fashion of war. At first the sight of the cross was sufficient to repel their attacks, but the only protection in the end was a circumvallation of straws, signed with the cross and fixed in the sand, around which the devils galloped for a while, and then retired, leaving the brethren to enjoy their victories and their repose".

This is a perfect example of the demonology of the period but hidden in it is probably a reference to the early inhabitants of the area, a few of whom had probably survived as primitive food gatherers, living along the sea shore. The monks, not understanding these people, turned them into demons.

Shortly after the death of Bartholomew the Convent of Durham turned the heritage of Farne into a permanent institution and sent two monks there, one of whom was called Magister or Custos and the other his Socius and the hermitage was called the House of Farne. The house became well endowed and comparatively wealthy. The records which have survived throw interesting light on the domestic economy of the monasteries in the Middle Ages. The monks exploited the agricultural fishing wealth of the islands. They grew crops, kept cattle, collected the birds' eggs, and caught the fish and seals which were found in abundance. Wrecks were a regular source of income. In 1357 they borrowed 40s. upon the credit of a wreck not yet broken up. In 1364 £4-5-7 was received from another wreck. Seals fetched a high price bearing in mind the value of money in those days. For six "celys" in 1371 they received 27s. 4d. In the same year they spent 45s. in buying a clock (horalogium), a rare treasure at that time.

In the fifteenth century the monks at Farne became very lax. In 1443 the master was dismissed for "pawning the best chalice and divers spoons, associating with ribalds and travelling over the country in garments rent, torn, and covered with mud". In 1461 John Kirke was rebuked for "haunting a womanse house over ofte a for noon and aftir".

In 1538 the monks of Farne ceased to exist as a corporation on the orders of Henry VIII, and the islands were handed over to the Dean and Chapter of Durham.

During the second half of the 16th and early 17th century the tower on the Inner Farne was used as a government fort similar to the one on Holy Island. In the reign of Charles II a lighthouse was established, consisting of a coal fire which was lit each night on top of Prior Castell's Tower. It was replaced in the 18th century by a beacon on the Brownsman. At last in 1809 a modern lighthouse with oil lights was established on the Inner Farne. In 1861 the Inner Group of the Farnes was sold by the Dean and Chapter to Archdeacon Thorpe and in 1894 the Outer Group passed into the hands of Lord Armstrong. All the islands were purchased in 1925 for the National Trust.

HERRING GULL *Larus argentatus* and
LESSER BLACK-BACKED GULL *Larus fuscus*

Gulls are the most common birds to be seen at the coast and are associated with the sea more than any other bird. Their cry is heard near any harbour when fish is being brought in or gutted, by the fishermen. The herring and lesser black-backed gulls are large gulls, having a five-foot wing span and being approximately twenty-one inches in length. They are the predators and scavengers of the islands, and are very aggressive. Vast numbers of eggs and young of other birds are stolen by them during the breeding season. They also scavenge fish and waste from harbours or boats and sewage from refuse tips found inland. Man's inefficient methods of disposing of his refuse have provided these birds with an abundance of food, thus helping this species to expand rapidly. The amount of food available is one of the controlling factors in the population of a species and as the gull is large and aggressive it is always the first to obtain any available food, so expanding the species in spite of efforts to control it. There have been cases of balanced bird reserves where all other species have been driven out and the reserve has been completely taken over by gulls. In the past local fishermen collected gulls eggs from the Farnes but now the control work is done by the wardens.

Nesting gulls cause problems by uprooting great quantities of vegetation, when building their large nests and if the eggs are lost they re-build, using more grass and plants. In the past large areas on certain islands have been denuded of vegetation by the gulls, leaving the soil exposed to wind erosion.

Fifty years ago the herring gull was quite rare but it now has the larger population of the two gulls. Over one thousand pairs of each species nest on the Farne Islands. Both these gulls can be identified by the colour of the upperparts of the wings, back and legs. The herring gull has pale-grey upperparts and flesh-pink legs and feet, while the lesser black-backed gull has dark-grey upperparts and yellow legs and feet. Both have white head, neck, tail and underparts and yellow beaks with a red spot on the lower bill. Juvenile birds are brown-flecked, growing darker as they mature, until at four years old they attain their adult plumage.

The birds are paired off before they arrive at their breeding sites but quarrels occur between males over territory and they will often tear up vegetation before beginning to fight. Display between the breeding couples is usually done by the droppings of the head between the feet, then raising the head upwards and calling loudly. Local vegetation or seaweed makes up the nest which is constructed on vegetation, bare soil, or bare rock, within the colony. The male often brings decorations in the form of flowers or shells, to the female, when she is sitting on her eggs. Three eggs form the clutch and the female sits for the first few days of incubation, as there is a days rest between each egg being laid. The eggs of the herring gull are pale brown blotched with dark brown and those of the lesser black-backed gull are pale brown to green, boldly spotted with dark brown. Incubation is shared until the chicks are hatched nearly twenty-five to twenty-seven days later, when both birds feed the chicks. The young are guided to where they will obtain food by the red spot on the lower bill. Experiments with cardboard beaks offered to young gulls have shown that the young will take no interest until a red spot is placed on the lower cardboard bill. Immediately interest is then taken and all the chicks reach up for food. The young are ready to fly after six weeks, having obtained their juvenile feathers during this time.

Herring gulls are resident and can be seen near the islands all the year round, although a small local dispersal does take place. The lesser black-backed gull is mainly migratory and moves southwards towards the equator for the winter months. Any lesser black-backed gulls seen during the winter months are probably birds from colonies further north.

FULMAR *Fulmar glacialis*

In spite of centuries of exploitation on St. Kilda (then the only breeding site of the fulmar in Great Britain), when crofters harvested the birds for food and oil and sold eggs to collectors, the fulmar population exploded and new colonies built up on the Scottish mainland and other islands till, fifty years later, they had spread right down the east coast of Scotland to Yorkshire. Fulmars were recorded in the vicinity of the Farnes during the summer of 1919, but it was not until 1935 that the first egg was found on Inner Farne. Since then there has been a very slow increase until in 1989 when 239 pairs were recorded nesting on the islands.

The fulmar is very similar to a gull in colouring and size but has a distinctive thick neck and a segmented bill, above which are two nostril tubes. These tubes are common to all the Petrel family, of which the fulmar is a member and in Scotland this bird is nicknamed "Tubenose". It is the only member of the petrel family breeding on the Farnes. The wings are long and narrow with grey upper surfaces and dark-grey primary feathers. The back and tail are pearl-grey and the underparts white. The legs are a bluish-flesh colour and the gape mauve. Perhaps the most fascinating thing about the fulmar is the way it glides effortlessly in flight, rarely flapping its wings and picking up the wind as it turns, often following the contours of the waves, before returning in a wide circle and gliding away again. There are two "phases" of fulmar, the one described above which breeds in this area and is referred to as the light phase, and the blue fulmar which has a blue-grey head and upperparts, and is referred to as the dark phase. The latter breed much further north, but do sometimes wander into the area during the winter months.

It has been suggested that the fulmar pairs for life. The nesting territory certainly attracts the same pair of birds in some cases. Courtship consists mainly of bill crossing and caressing of heads.

A cliff nesting species, it occupies its nest early, always settling on high ledges from which it can launch itself straight into the air, as it finds difficulty in rising from flat ground. The nest is a scrape on a cliff ledge, slightly hollowed if there is any soil on it. At the beginning of the incubation period the fulmar is a shy bird and is easily disturbed from its nest and slow to return, thus its egg is often left unattended and is predated by gulls. The female lays one roughly-textured white egg which it will not replace that season if lost. Incubation is done by both birds in turn and it takes from fifty-five to fifty-seven days for the egg to hatch. The chick is fed by both parents for anything up to fifty-seven days, by regurgitation, until they consider the fledgeling old enough to start feeding itself. When this time is reached they stop feeding the chick but continue to fly past the ledge, encouraging it to leave. It is very reluctant to do this but eventually hunger forces it to launch into the air for its very first flight down to the sea to feed.

Later in the incubation period, when a stronger association with the egg or young has developed, if anything or anyone approaches too close to the nest, the bird will take up the defensive attitude of head wagging and mouth opening prior to ejecting a spurt of evil-snelling oil from the mouth, which can reach a distance of up to four feet.

The fulmar feeds mainly on fish offal and plankton from which it produces the oil to feed its young. The plankton is obtained at night when it rises to the surface of the water.

By mid-September the nesting places are usually deserted and forty years ago no fulmars would be found near the islands during September to November, but now only some of the birds disperse over the oceans and each year more birds stay in the vicinity of their nesting sites, as competition for nesting sites grows.

PUFFIN *Fratercula arctica*

The most unusual seabird nesting on the Farnes, both in appearance and habit, is the puffin. Its large triangular bill often causes it to be called the "Sea Parrot", while local fishermen refer to it as "Tommy Noddy". This member of the auk family is more designed for swimming on and under the water than for flying and its rapid wing beat in flight always gives the impression that the puffin is just managing to keep in the air.

The puffin is twelve inches in length and is easily recognised during the breeding season by its brightly coloured striped bill with yellow rosettes at the angle of the gape, black crown and upperparts, grey cheeks, blue horny plates above and below the eyes, white underparts and bright orange legs and feet. After the breeding season, the blue horny plates, yellow rosettes and outer skin of the bill are all shed leaving the puffin with a smaller, duller bill. Both the male and female are alike in appearance.

Visitors often look for puffin nests and are surprised when they cannot find them among those of other birds. This is because the puffin nests underground in old disused rabbit burrows or in holes excavated by them with their large powerful beaks. The burrows are usually three to five feet in length, varying in depth according to the depth of soil available. On one of the islands, wreckage from a wooden ship provides tunnels about nine inches square and the puffins use these as artificial burrows.

Puffins first visit the islands during February and March as though checking on their nesting sites. They return in early April to claim their burrows and defend them against other would-be occupiers. During this period pairs of puffins can be so engrossed in fighting over the ownership of a burrow, that one can approach within inches of them without being noticed. As the birds are usually paired off before arriving at the breeding site, the only courtship display seen on the land is occasional bill shaking and bowing. Puffins normally lay only one egg (on rare occasions they have been known to lay two) and this is incubated by both the birds in turn, for a period of forty-one to forty-three days before the chick is hatched out.

Both the parents feed the chick and can be seen entering the burrow with several sand eels or small fry in their beaks. The fish are usually lined up in the beak with all the heads on one side and the tails at the other. Approximately forty days later the young are deserted by the parents and after being without food for a few days, they are forced to emerge from their burrows. They do this at night and fly away from the islands to fend for themselves on the sea. This is the reason you never see a young puffin on, or near, the island.

Puffins have a lot of predators waiting to steal their catch of fish while they are carrying it back to feed their young. Common and roseate terns can often be seen diving at puffins which are just surfacing with a bill full of fish, forcing them to submerge again. They repeat this so often that the puffin is forced to surrender its catch. Landing on the islands is just as perilous for the puffin as he has to avoid lesser black-backed and herring gulls which wait near the entrance to his burrow and force him to drop the fish. However, observations made at two separate colonies, one where predation of food was heavy and the other where little or no predation took place, showed that the fledgeling puffins in both colonies were of similar weight. This would seem to imply that the adults must compensate for any loss of food. Predation also takes place when gulls seize young puffins which venture too near to the entrance of the burrow.

If puffins burrow in shallow soil, difficulties may arise following a period of dry weather. During such a period the vegetation dies off, exposing the soil to the elements. Rain can then quickly percolate between the soil particles flooding the burrow beneath. Thus any eggs present are chilled, whilst any chicks are forced to flee out of the burrow only to be picked off as they emerge, by waiting gulls.

The first full count of this species in 1971 found that approximately 11,000 pairs of puffins were breeding on the Farnes and regular counting since has shown a steady increase in numbers, reaching 26,500 pairs in 1989. The main colonies being on Inner Farne, The Wideopens, Staple and Brownsman. The birds are present on and around the islands from February to mid August when they leave to spend the winter months on the oceans.

Donald Grisbleton.

RAZORBILL *Alca torda*

Although there has been a long history of razorbills breeding on the Farne Islands, it has never been a common bird and only a few pairs have managed to breed successfully each year. Being shy they are very easily disturbed from their nests and gulls soon pick off the unprotected egg. Numbers have increased very slowly and there are now ninety six pairs breeding. No doubt the constant protection they now receive will help this species to expand slowly in the future.

Razorbills can be confused with guillemots as they both have the same upright penguine-like stance and appearance. However the razorbill, which is sixteen inches in length, can be identified by its black upperparts and legs, white breast and deep blunt-ended bill crossed midway by a white line. In flight a white wing bar contrasts sharply with the black upper surfaces. During the breeding season adult razorbills have a white line extending from the base of the bill to the eye and the whole of the head and neck are black, weheras in the winter the front and sides of the neck and the lower sides of the head are white. Juvenile birds resemble adults in winter plumage but their bills are small and black and their legs are brown.

Courtship takes place on the water and early in the year small groups of razorbills may be seen swimming in line, then turning to form a circle, with beaks raised, and back into line again. On the nesting ledges, couples rub bills together and one bird may raise its head upwards, with beak open, while the partner nibbles and caresses its neck.

In mid-May a single egg, on rare occasions two, is laid in a crevice on a ledge of bare rock. The egg colour varies from pale fawn or white to green, blotched with brown and black. Both birds incubate the egg in turn, for a period of approximately thirty days, when the chick is hatched out, and is fed by both the parents. After bringing small fish to the chick for a period of at least fourteen days, by which time the young is well feathered, the parents then coax the chick down to the sea. The parents have been seen to push the chick off the ledge, then accompany it down to the water. Although there are records at other colonies of parents assisting the young birds down to the sea by holding the young bird's wing tips in their bills, no such observations have been made at the Farnes. It may be possible that as the sea is directly below the ledges and the young birds can therefore fall into the water without striking rocks, that assistance is not given.

Once on the water the parents continue to feed their young until they become independent, and young razorbills follow their parents begging for food by making a mewing call. When feeding, the razorbill swallows the fish while underwater, but when feeding their young they carry the fish crosswise in the beak, avoiding gulls who are always waiting to steal their catch. This bird is capable of catching up to twelve small fish and holding them all in the beak at the same time.

The flight of the razorbill is typical of the auk family, direct with rapid wing beats. When alighting on their breeding ledges they sweep upwards towards the ledge with their feet spread out controlling their landing speed with their wings. Like all members of the auk family they are expert swimmers, using their small wings to propel them forward underwater and their feet as rudders to assist them in turning while pursuing their prey. When swimming on top of the water they use their webbed feet as paddles. They are not as expert, however, at walking, moving mostly on their tarus (foreleg) in a most ungainly manner, their legs having evolved more for swimming.

The nesting sites are usually deserted by mid-August, the birds having dispersed mainly southwards from their breeding grounds. In winter months the birds feed and roost on the sea.

CORMORANT *Phalacrorax carbo*

A large black bird, thirty-six inches in length, which swims low in the water with its long neck held erect. On land it stands holding out its wings to dry as does its near relative, the shag, with whom it is often confused. The cormorant can be distinguished from the shag because it is larger in size, has brownish-black plumage, white chin and cheeks, long hooked bill and during the breeding season, a white thigh patch which can be seen in flight. The male bird displays these thigh patches to the female by flapping its wings and standing with wings outstretched. The female responds by pointing its hooked bill upwards and holding its tail erect. The cormorant's flight is swift, direct and usually close to the water, with neck and legs fully extended. The immature birds are dark brown and have white cheeks, chin and breast.

In spite of its large size the cormorant is a shy bird which nests in colonies for protection and, if disturbed from its nest and eggs, will unfortunately stand by while gulls devour its eggs. The cormorant makes a large nest composed mainly of seaweed and sometimes decorated with plants. It is continually adding to its nest and can be seen trailing seaweed up to six feet in length, for this purpose. The eggs are laid from the end of April to late May and clutch can be anything from one to six eggs, but three or four are more usual. They are large and appear to have an uneven, whitish chalk deposited on top of a pale blue shell. Incubation is done by both the birds and takes approximately twenty-eight days. When the chicks hatch out they are completely naked, blind and very ugly. This is quite unusual in the marine bird world as most of these birds hatch out with a complete covering of down on their bodies and their eyes open. Within a few days, however, down grows, the eyes open and later juvenile feathers appear through the down. Both parents feed the young with regurgitated, partially-digested fish passed from mouth to mouth and during the breeding season, while the young are being fed, the smell of decaying fish carries for a considerable distance from the cormorant colony. After a month of being fed in or near the nest, the fledgelings move off on to the sea where they feed mainly on fish and small crabs.

It is fascinating to watch cormorants fishing. Sometimes they leap completely out of the water before diving for their prey, or catch fish unawares by quietly submerging. Often they can be seen holding their heads underwater looking for fish which they bring to the surface, and beating the larger fish on the water until they are subdued enough to be swallowed whole. In China, cormorants are used to catch fish for man, being tethered by the neck and then forced to give up any fish caught. Underwater it uses its feet to propel forward but rarely stays under for more than one minute. The cormorant does not rest upon the water as ducks do, but makes for the land. When alarmed it will completely submerge its body and neck leaving only its eye and beak out of the water.

A colony has been recorded nesting on the Megstone for the last three hundred years until this island was deserted in 1973. Over the last fifty years another colony has been breeding at the North Wamses and in 1981 a small colony was established on East Wideopen. Numbers on the Megstone rose to about 300 pairs by 1946 but breeding success depended very much on the weather conditions as the whole colony could be washed off when violent sea storms occurred during the nesting season. Even though the birds are now breeding on more sheltered islands numbers have remained static. This species winters on inland waters where they are thought to do great damage to fresh water fishing stocks and in the past the local salmon fisheries put a price of twenty-five pence on their heads and shooting them became a profitable pastime, however this reward has been withdrawn but it is obvious that this shooting is still continuing and curtailing any rise in the population."

The cormorant is mainly a resident bird, although a large number of the first-year birds do disperse up and down the coast and occasionally cross from the east to the west. The older birds remain in home waters.

Donald E Malick

EIDER *Somateria mollissima*

Because of its association with St. Cuthbert, who protected this bird and gave it his blessing during his stay on Inner Farne from 676 to 687, the eider is perhaps the most famous of all the island's birds, and even to-day is known locally as "Cuddy's Duck". Twenty-three inches in length, the eider can be distinguished from most other ducks because it is larger and has an unusual head profile. The bill forms a straight line from the top of the head and gives the head a triangular shape. Male and female eiders have quite different plumage. The female is drab in appearance with brown feathers barred with black, which help to camouflage her while she is on the nest. The male however has quite a brilliant plumage with black belly, white back and white head capped with a black crown. Added to this a bright green patch on the nape of the neck, a pink breast and yellowish green bill make this a most striking drake. This breeding plumage stays from November to the end of June when the drake moults and takes on a dull plumage of black with small white patches. It is nearly five years before the male eider achieves full breeding plumage.

Mating starts as early as December and the birds continue displaying and pairing off until April or May, when they gather round the islands in large numbers. The drake displays during courtship by pressing the bill down to touch the breast, then jerking the head upright and calling to the female "coo-roo-ah". The male often accompanies the female ashore when searching for a nesting site, which is a hollow in the ground or amongst vegetation. While settling in on her new nest she will indicate to her attendant drake, by pointing her beak and hissing at certain objects around the nest which she would like removed. He does his best to tidy up the area to her liking. The duck then lines her nest with down plucked from her breast and whenever she leaves the nest she will first cover the eggs with this down to keep them warm and protect them from would-be predators. The drake may attend for a day or two to see if the duck is settled, before leaving her to join the other males. The males then go through their prolonged moult and large rafts of moulting drakes assemble in the Firth of Forth and smaller rafts just off the Northumbrian mainland.

The duck lays four to six eggs and occasionally up to ten eggs, which she incubates for twenty-seven to twenty-nine days, only leaving the nest for short periods to take water and a little food. The eggs are large and olive green to buff in colour. Some ducks never leave their nest at all and live off their body fat, thus reducing their weight from four and a half to two and a half pounds. Very large clutches of fifteen to twenty-four eggs have been found, but these are the result of more than one bird laying in the same nest.

When the ducklings are hatched out and dry, the duck takes them down to the sea for the next suitable tide, which will help take them over to the mainland, where they feed near the shore. The ducklings are quite independent feeders when hatched out and are safer on the sea, where they can dive to safety from attacking gulls.

Although the male eider does not attend the female after the first few days, other non-breeding eider ducks are always there to help her to escort and look after her chicks. These non-breeding ducks are aptly called "Aunties" and can often be seen helping to accompany large numbers of chicks on the sea.

Eiders nest on most of the islands, with the largest colonies on Inner Farne and Brownsman. Numbers were reduced during the war years and there were less than one hundred ducks nesting in 1945. Constant protection since then has allowed the numbers to build up gradually until recent years have seen between 1,200 and 1,750 ducks nesting.

In some countries the edier is exploited for its famous down. After she has lined her nest, the down is removed by the collectors and she must then re-line the nest. This is repeated two or three times before she is allowed to settle down and incubate her eggs.

Although the females have generally left the islands by about mid-July, ducks can be seen on the water near the islands most of the year.

THE KETTLE

St. Cuthbert's Gut

Prior Castell's Tower

Churn Gut

Farne Haven
St. Cuthbert's Cove

St. Cuthbert's Chapel

The Churn

Garden

Fish House Ruins

Site of Low Lighthouse

Wideopen Gut

London Rock

FARNE ISLAND
OR
INNER FARNE

High Lighthouse
Site of Cross

Black Rock

The Stack

Pinnacles

OXSCAR or
SOUTH GOLDSTONE

GLORORUM SI

SWEDMAN

ELBOW

MEGSTONE

ISLESTO

INNER

SOUND

St. Cuthbert's Chapel

KNOCKS REEF

SOLAN ROCK

The Kettle

ST CUTHBERT'S GUT

FARNE ISLAND
OR INNER FARNE

High Water Mark

Low Water Mark

KNIVESTONE

NORTHERN HARES

LONGSTONE

SUNDERLAND HOLE

Wreck of Forfarshire
1838

CLOVE CAR

LONGSTONE
END

X

LITTLE
HARCAR

BLUE CAPS

NORTH WAMSES

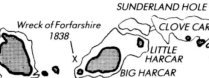

BIG HARCAR

RODDAM & GREEN

SOUTH WAMSES

NAMELESS ROCK

BROWNSMAN

The Longstone

GUN ROCK

STAPLE ISLAND

PINNACLES

SKENEY SCAR

CALLERS

CRUMSTONE

STAPLE SOUND

THE

FANG

FARNE ISLANDS

0	¼	½	¾	1 mile

SCALE

LITTLE SCARCAR

BIG SCARCAR

THE BUSH

RINGED PLOVER *Charadrius hiaticula*

This small, plump, attractive wader breeds on the Farne Islands annually and ten to twenty pairs have been recorded each year. Numbers seem to have changed little over the last one hundred years. The ringed plover also breeds on the mainland but with the increase in the number of tourists, there are less quiet areas available for this beautiful little wader. At the Farnes, they nest mainly on Inner Farne, Staple and Brownsman, as there are few predators on these islands. Nearly every nest is closely associated with a tern colony and it is obvious that these waders are using the terns as a shelter against predators. If any predators approach a tern colony they are immediatelly mobbed by a crowd of very aggressive terns. The ringed plover's main protection is, of course, its colouring and when it is sitting very still it is extremely difficult to see. The eggs are mainly buff-coloured tinged with grey and spotted with brown, black and grey blotches. These colours fade when the eggs are exposed to the sunlight, while the nest is left unattended.

The ringed plover can be identified by its small (seven and a half inches in length) plump shape and rapid running movements when feeding. It has brown upperparts, white underparts and a broad black band across its breast. The legs are yellow-orange and the orange bill is tipped with black. The crown of the head is brown, a white collar surrounds the neck and a black mark passes below the eye. A prominent white forehead shows above the bill and in flight a narrow white bar stretches across the wing.

The food of the ringed plover is chiefly small marine insects, worms and shellfish found on the shore near the water's edge. Most other waders keep their heads down when feeding and searching for food, but the ringed plover runs quickly from one spot to another with its head only slightly lowered, pausing for a moment every few yards to pick up food by tilting the whole body forward on the legs without stretching out its neck and head.

When displaying during courtship the birds fly slowly in pairs, close to the ground, passing in front of, or twisting towards, each other, at the same time rapidly repeating three single shrill notes. The most unusual display is done when the nest or young are approached by man. The parent bird will then fly a short distance away and pretend to be injured by trailing or dragging a leg in an effort to distract attention away from the nest or young. It then appears to recover and flies down.

The next consists simply of a scrape in the ground, shingle, sand or earth, which is sometimes decorated with shells and small pebbles placed around the edge. The normal clutch is four eggs and the colours of the eggs provides an extremely good cmaouflage being buff to grey, spotted with brown and black. The first nests are made in April or earlier if the weather is suitable, and both the parents share the incubating of the eggs, changing quite frequently. After twenty-five days the chicks are hatched and within a day or two they have been removed from the nest by the parents and hidden in various places nearby. Both the parents then have a busy time feeding the separated chicks, but by this separation their chances of survival are heightened, as a predator may see one move but the movement does not lead him to the whole brood. If predators are near the parent birds give an alarm call and the chicks freeze, making it difficult to distinguish them from their surroundings. The parents continue to feed the young until they are independent when they start to nest again. It is usual for the ringed plover to have two broods per year and cases of three broods have been known, especially when a brood of eggs has been lost.

The ringed plover is classed as a summer visitor, as the local birds disperse southwards. Their places are taken by birds which have bred further north and flocks of up to twenty birds can often be seen during the winter months on the deserted beaches on the mainland.

Ronald Embleton

SHAG *Phalacrocorax aristotelis*

At first sight the shag is often confused with its near relative the cormorant, and is sometimes referred to as the "green cormorant" but close study will soon reveal that both in appearance and habit is quite different.

The shag's plumage is greenish-black and during the breeding season it shows a fine curved crest of feathers on its head. A brilliant sea-green eye is prominent about its long, black, hooked bill which when opened, displays a bright, orange-yellow gape. The immature shags, however, are all brown and at this stage can easily be confused with an immature cormorant.

The usual voice of the shag is a loud rasping croak, but when defending the nest it produces a deep grunt and a loud hissing noise.

In its special display to the male, the female throws back her neck turning the head from side to side, at the same time vibrating the loose skin of the throat and cheeks and holding the tail erect. She then darts the head forward quickly at the male, opening the beak to display her bright yellow gape. The male responds by stretching its neck and raising its beak. Head shaking and beak opening is also used as a threat against intruders.

The shag is more aggressive than the cormorant and can defend its nest against all intruders. Being aggressive, it does not need to nest in large colonies for protection and it is much more widely distributed among the islands, nesting where suitable terrain occurs, and guillemots, razorbills, fulmars and kittiwakes.

Nest building commences, if the weather is good, as early as February, when a large nest is constructed on a broad ledge, using seaweed and vegetation, or old nests are repaired and used again if they have survived the winter's storms. Stealing of nesting material is a common occurrence during this period and it is necessary for one parent bird to defend the nest while the partner collects building material. Normally two or three eggs are laid from mid-April onwards and they take from twenty-four to twenty-eight days to hatch, but if nests containing eggs or young are washed away by violent seas, the bird will rebuild and late broods in August and September are not unusual. The eggs are pale blue, covered unevenly with a white chalky deposit which stains easily.

The chicks are born blind and naked, as is the cormorant, but after a few days the eyes open and a covering of down grows on the body. One parent broods the youngsters continuously, during this period, shading them during hot weather and keeping them warm on cooler days, while the other parent sees to all the feeding by regurgitating partially-digested food into the mouths of the young. When the chicks have grown, both the parents share the feeding duties until the young are strong enough to accompany their parents on the sea.

They feed mainly on fish, diving and chasing their prey underwater and propelling themselves forward with their feet and wings. Before surfacing they raise the head and neck out of the water to ensure there is no danger. A characteristic feature of both the shag and the cormorant is the way they spread out their wings to dry in the wind while resting on the rocks, but unlike the cormorant the shag is rarely seen on freshwater.

Although there had been occasional records of shags nesting on the islands, it was not until 1931 onwards that the shag nested annually. Numbers increased each year until by 1966 approximately three hundred and sixty pairs were recorded, but in 1968 a major disaster in the form of a dinoflagellate eruption (sometimes called Red Tide) resulted in the loss, through poisoning, of eighty per cent of the breeding population). Numbers have increased dramatically reaching 1,686 pairs by 1989.

In winter there is some dispersal of the younger shags but the majority stay in the vicinity of the islands or coastline all the year round.

OYSTERCATCHER *Haematopus ostralegus*

A very noisy, excitable but wary wader, the oystercatcher is one of the most attractive birds breeding on the Farnes. Approximately twenty-five pairs breed there each year, with the largest concentration breeding on Brownsman.

Large in size, being seventeen inches in length with black and white plumage, very prominent large orange-red bill and long pink legs, it is easily recognised even from a distance. When in flight a broad white bar can be seen stretching across the wing and a broad black terminal band on the end of the white tail. Because of this pied appearance it is sometimes known as the "Sea Pie". The male and female are alike in appearance.

They feed on mussels and limpets, caught while the tide is ebbing and the shellfish are still wet and off guard. The oystercatcher opens the mussel by giving it a sharp blow with its beak, at the joint of the shells, which jars the shells slightly apart. It can then insert the beak and lever the shells open. The beak is powerful enough to break up the shell with a few hard blows. Limpets are dislodged by the oystercatcher after a blow on the edge of the shell which either removes it completely or at least sufficiently for the beak to be inserted to lever it off the rock. They often do this levering with a rotary action and the bird can be seen walking round its prey as it dislodges it. The oystercatcher also feeds off worms and insects found in the sand and mud on the coast, or among the soil in ploughed fields further inland.

Whenever danger threatens, or when excited, the bird pushes his head and neck forward, at the same time pointing the bill downwards and piping continously. During courtship some piping takes place while the bird runs with short quick steps in various directions. Later, when the female is sitting on the nest, the male will circle overhead using a slow wing beat in flight and piping as it flies.

A scrape on the ground is their only nest, near the shore among boulders, stones, shingle, sand or vegetation. No nesting material is used but the perimeter of the scrape is sometimes decorated with shells, pebbles or plants. The eggs are large and out of all proportion to the size of the bird, but this allows the chicks to develop fully within the shells and enables them to be mobile immediately they are hatched, as the nest offers no protection.

The clutch is normally three eggs laid in mid-May and incubation starts when the last egg is laid. The eggs are perfectly camouflaged, being pale stone or yellow brown with brown-black markings, and are extremely difficult to find. This protects the eggs when they are left in the nest unattended. Both birds incubate the eggs but the female does the greater share. If the nesting bird is approached early during the incubation period, it will slip off the nest and run silently for a good distance before taking flight and giving voice to warn its mate. Later, as the association with the nest and eggs becomes stronger, the bird becomes quite bold and aggressive towards intruders, diving and mobbing them until they depart. The incubation period varies according to the weather and the number of times the bird is disturbed from the nest. When disturbed, the bird will desert the nest for a considerable period, leaving the eggs to incubate in the warmth of the day. Should there be a cold spell, incubation is delayed so that the period varies between twenty-four and twenty-seven days.

When the chicks are hatched out they stay in the nest for two days; then they are hidden by the parents in different places in order to increase their chances of survival. They are fed by both parents until they can fend for themselves and after the breeding season the birds feed together in flocks, some moving southwards to their winter feeding area. Large flocks can be found during the winter, in and around estuaries where there are large amounts of shellfish available. Small flocks can be seen near the islands and the adjacent coastline, most of the year.

GUILLEMOT *Uria aalge*

This bird is the main victim of oil pollution at sea, countless numbers of oiled and dead guillemots have been washed onto our shores and the pathetic sight of those still alive stirred mans conscience to try towards improving the environment. As losses can be very high during an oiling incident any breeding sites used by this species must be carefully protected. At the Farnes there is one of the finest colonies in the country and the sight of the crowded Pinnacle Rocks just off Staple Island, is now world famous. The first count of this species at the Farnes was made in 1971 when 1,686 pairs were found to be breeding, since that date the regular monitoring shows a very welcome rise in the population reaching the staggering figure of almost 14,000 pairs by 1988. This increase is partly due to the increased protection they have received at the Farnes by restricting visitor access to certain cliff tops on Staple Island.

The guillemot is sixteen and a half inches in height and has an upright stance when on land. From a distance it appears to have a black and white plumage during the breeding season, but when examined more closely one can see that the head, throat and upperparts of the body and wings are chocolate brown and the underparts white. The beak is slender and pointed and the legs and feet pale brown. Some of the birds have a white ring around the eye which extends back across the face. These are bridled guillemots but no one knows what causes this difference in appearance, as bridled parents do not necessarily produce bridled young and non-bridled parents can produce bridled young. Four per cent of the guillemots at the Farnes are bridled and it is interesting to note that the colonies further north have as greater proprtion of bridled birds than those in the south. After moulting during the period July to November, the upperparts of the bird change to grey-brown with the throat and face cheeks white, except for a small black line extending backwards across the face from the eye. The winter plumage of the juvenile birds is similar to that of the adults, except for the fact that they have a smaller bill.

Periodically during the winter months and early spring, vast numbers of guillemots assemble at their breeding grounds. They cover the top of the Pinnacles and when a boat approaches they peel off the nearest stack, flying in a huge circle before returning to the Pinnacles, the first bird arriving just as the last is taking off.

In the spring, when the colony is established, the guillemot becomes a most excitable bird, always moving, bobbing, squabbling with neighbours, showing an interest in other birds and generally making a tremendous noise with its loud raucous calls. The tops of the Pinnacles and surrounding ledges are covered with guillemots and finding a place to land becomes so difficult they have to hover above like helicopters, before dropping into position.

Affectionate displays between couples is constant. Bowing, neck craning and head nibbling is quite common. Occasionally, pairs and even single birds run their beaks down their breast then jerk their head upwards and shake the beak from side to side.

No nest is made. The single egg which varies in colour from white, to blue, to brown marked with brown or black blotches, is simply laid on the bare rock. The shape of the egg is such, being very bulbous at one end and pointed at the other, that when knocked it will not roll far but rather revolves. Both the birds incubate the egg in turn and the egg is held on top of the webbed feet and covered with loose skin from the rear of the bird, which it pulls over with its beak. Incubation takes approximately thirty-two days and at first the young chick is brooded under one of the parent's wings, while the other bird collects food. When well-feathered and about half-grown the chick is coaxed down on to the water where both the parents continue to feed it. By the end of July the nesting sites are nearly cleared with only a few late nesters still lingering on. Dispersal is generally away from the breeding grounds and the birds spend the winter months feeding and roosting on the sea.

KITTIWAKE *Rissa tridactyla*

The kittiwake is a true sea-going gull, as outside the breeding season it spends most of its time on the sea. It can be identified immediately by its unmistakable call "Kitti-wa-ake", which it repeats constantly. This is our smallest breeding gull, being sixteen inches in length and the only British breeding gull with black legs. In appearance both the male and female are alike. The back and upper wing surfaces are grey and the black wing tips look as though they have been dipped in ink. The remainder of the plumage is white and its beak a lemon yellow. The gape, when opened, is a bright orange to attract the very young birds to their food supply. It is interesting to notice the legs and feet of the very young birds, which are extremely large and appear to be out of proportion to the size of the body. The reason for this is that when the chick is hatched, its legs and feet are fully grown.

This delightful gull breeds in colonies on cliff faces and ledges, often mixing with shags and guillemots. Any small projection on a cliff face is used as a base for a nest, which is made of vegetation and seaweed mixed with mud, but some birds, thought to be young ones, build nests too low on the cliffs and spring storms wash the nest away. The nesting site is defended against all other intruders and fights do occur when interlopers try to take possession of a nest. Probably the most spectacular nesting site is on Staple island where a deep fissure in the rock (known as "Kittiwake Gully"), provides plenty of ledges for nesting. During the breeding season one can stand within a few feet of the nesting birds and observe the tremendous activity and noise which surrounds a colony of this type. From the boat one can also see a large colony of kittiwakes at Pinnacles Haven on Brownsman island.

Paired birds seem to have a great affection for each other, and can often be seen crossing bills and gently caressing each other's heads and necks. They lay two or three eggs and these vary in colour from pale blue-grey to yellow, marked with brown and grey blotches. Both the male and female birds incubate the eggs for a period of twenty-one to twenty-four days, when the young birds are hatched out. Once again great affection is shown between the birds whenever they change over the incubation duty, and displays sometimes takes four to five minutes before the actual changeover is made. The young birds are born covered with soft down and after four to five weeks they are fully fledged and ready to fly. During this period the fledglings are fed by both parents with regurgitated, partially-digested fish. Nesting as they do on small ledges on cliffs, one would fear for the safety of the chicks but they seem to have an inborn instinct to stay in the nest.

The immature kittiwake has a distinctive plumage and as it was once thought to be a different species, was called the "Tarrock". This name still applies to the immature kittiwake, which has colouring similar to the adult, but with extra dark bands diagonally over the upper surface of the wings, which give a zig-zagged effect, a dark collar on the neck and a dark band on the tail feathers.

By the end of August the nests are deserted, but the kittiwakes can still be seen around the islands most of the winter. Young birds seem to spend the first two to three years travelling over the oceans as far away as Newfoundland, Greenland, Iceland and southwards to France and Spain, before returning to start breeding at the Farnes.

Kittiwakes do not scavenge for their food as do other gulls, but feed off small fish and crustacea.

The predators of the kittiwakes' eggs are the lesser black-backed gull and the herring gull which swoop in on unattended nests and carry off the eggs. With constant protection over the last forty years, however, the number of kittiwakes has increased and is still increasing. There are now (1990) 5,800 pairs of kittiwakes nesting on eleven of the islands.

ROSEATE TERN *Sterna dougalli*

This species, which in Britain, is at the northern limit of its range, has suffered a severe decline in breeding numbers throughout the British Isles from a peak of over 3,000 pairs in the 1970s to less than 500 pairs in 1989. The same level of decline has been seen at the Farnes, dropping from an average of 90 pairs throughout the 1970s to a low of 3 pairs in 1983 recovering to 21 pairs in 1988. An occasional pair still breed at Inner Farne and they can sometimes be seen among the mid-day roost of arctic terns on the rocks just south of the landing jetty. One can pick them out by their black bill with a little red at the base, red legs and very long tail streamers extending beyond the folded wings. In full breeding plumage the breast has a beautiful rosy tinge, hence the name "roseate" but this is only present for a short period of time. The white forehead appears with the winter plumage and the bill turns completely black. The roseate is the last of the four species to arrive at the end of May.

TERNS

Although they arrive at different times most of the terns settle down to nest at the end of May or early June. Availability of food is the main controlling factor which governs the start of the nesting and should the weather be cold and small fry and sand eels not available, the nesting will be delayed.

Prior to nesting, aerial displays are performed. Pairs of birds climb high into the air, then glide down with wings fully extended, keeping the same distance apart, side-slipping and spiralling to the ground. Later, when a male occupies a territory, he flies around with a fish in his beak as though trying to attract a mate. When paired the male walks round the sitting female, with his wings partially outstretched and his tail elevated, offering her the fish, which she accepts.

The tern's nest consists of a scrape among rocks, sand or vegetation, made in large colonies, the roseate tern prefering natural hollows under rocks or tussocks of grass. Sandwich, arctic and roseate have a normal clutch of two eggs and the common tern three eggs. All are incubated by both the parent birds and whichever bird is not on incubation duty, feeds the sitting bird. Tern's eggs are variable in colour, with the ground colour varying from buff to brown and sometimes green, blotched with dark brown. Incubation takes twenty-one days and the young are fed by both the parents with whole fish and sand eels carried in the bill to the nest. The whole fish is passed from the parent to the chick and sometimes small chicks can be seen trying to swallow fish as long as themselves. A cold wet spell at this stage can cause high mortality among the young, as cold weather causes a scarcity of fish and heavy rain soaks the vegetation among which the chicks shelter.

Sandwich terns, when half grown, gather together in large groups and 'troop' round the island followed by the parents, vainly attempting to feed their own young.

All juvenile birds resemble their parents in winter plumage and leave their nesting area during early to mid-August. They feed around the islands and along the adjacent coast until September, when they begin their long migration to the southern hemisphere, to enjoy another summer. Ringed terns are regularly recovered from the west and south coasts of Africa but one young arctic tern was found exhausted and dying on a beach near Melbourne, Australia, a distance of 11,000 miles, 115 days after it had been ringed as a nestling on the Farnes on 25th June 1982.

TERNS

One of the most exciting moments of the year is the arrival of the terns on the islands. These summer visitors are a welcome sight as they herald the beginning of another season. Terns are sometimes called "sea swallows" as they resemble the swallow in shape, having long pointed wings and a deeply forked tail. They migrate like a swallow, spending our winters in the southern hemisphere and so enjoying two summers each year. There are four species of terns nesting on the Farne Islands, common, sandwich, artic and roseate. The geographical position of the Farne Islands is such that there is an overlap of nesting areas of terns. The islands are at the southern limit of the artic tern, the northern limit of the roseate tern and in the central range of the common and sandwich tern.

The terns are easily picked out by their buoyant flight, narrow pointed wings, deeply forked tails, thin bills, always held pointing downwards in flight, and their constant diving into the sea for food. The terns nesting on the Farnes all have grey upper wing surfaces, whitish underparts and tail and, during the breeding season, black caps on their heads.

SANDWICH TERN *Sterna sandvicensis*

The sandwich terns are the first to arrive at the beginning of April, although some of the first birds seen are on passage to more northerly breeding areas. This is the largest of the four terns, being sixteen inches in length, and can be recognised by the short forked tail, black legs and long black bill tipped with yellow. During the spring and early summer the crown of the head is completely black and the feathers at the rear of the head protrude like a shaggy crest, from the back of the head, especially when the bird is excited. During mid-summer, even when still sitting on eggs, the bird commences moulting and the forehead becomes white. Colonies often vary in size each year and often change their breeding islands but the trend during the 1970 – 1990 period at the Farnes is slowly upwards with between 1,500 – 4,000 pairs nesting at either Brownsman Island or Inner Farne.

COMMON TERN *Sterna hirundo*

Common terns arrive at the beginning of May with the artic terns and they nest within an artic tern colony. Their name would suggest that they are numerous but there is only a small colony at the Farnes which has increased from 100 to 300+ pairs in the last twenty years. Fourteen inches in length, the common tern is the smallest of the four species nesting on the islands. In breeding plumage it has a red bill with a black tip, red legs and the tail streamers are much longer than those of the sandwich terns, but shorter than those of the arctic. In winter the tern has a white forehead and the bill darkens, leaving only a little red at the base of the lower mandible.

ARCTIC TERN *Sterna paradisea*

Arctic terns are fifteen inches in length and can be identified by their blood-red bill, red legs, deeply forked tail, long tail streamers and very aggressive attitude during the breeding season. Again the white forehead soon appears and later the legs and bill turn black. The arctic terns, which arrive at the beginning of May, nest both at Brownsman Island and Inner Farne with sometimes a small colony at Staple Island. Between 1970 and 1990 the number of breeding pairs has increased from just over 1,000 pairs to approximately 4,000 pairs. It is wonderful to witness what is known as a "dread", when the colony suddenly falls silent and then soars into the air and out to sea in a great wheeling flight, before returning to the land and their incessant chattering again.